Poems From a Soulful Heart

Part One

By Vala Boyd

For my boys…. May you always chase your dreams and discover new things.

~Love Mama

Dragon Betrayer

You watch me as I die

You, sing a victory song

You have slaughtered what was left of us

You pump your fist in the air

You dance your victory dance

You have betrayed us

You have defied us

You have lost the trust that we had in you

You are no longer our chosen one

You are the betrayer of the dragons

You shall no longer rule with us

You have killed us all

<u>Butterfly</u>

You are majestic

When you fly

You are full of life

You fly the way you want

You do not take life for granted

You have so many colors on your wings

You are sweet and kind

You are shy and keep to your self

You are a butterfly

Elemental Lover

He caresses my skin with such expertise

Memorizing yet already knowing every inch
of my being

He engulfs me in warm waves that slowly
but skillfully run down my body causing me
to tremble with glee

His embrace is well needed at the end of
each day

His calming effect like a lullaby sending me
into sleep

Our Love is unknown but not forbidden

His elemental status granting him privilege
to do as he pleases

He calls for me each night, beckoning me to
bathe in him

He is my Elemental Lover, for Water is his
name.

Filled With Nothing

My mind won't shut off, so I allow the numbness to take root and freeze my being to the core.

My body does what I need it to yet feelings are hard to ignore so I turn off the warmth and embrace the cold.

It engulfs me like a blanket of smooth ice.

Leading me to peace and lack of thought.

Thank You my cool cunning friend for taking me away from the warmth of memories and ideas.

Do not worry I will not stay here for long, just long enough to do what I must before the ice shatters to tiny pieces around my warming body.

For now I will embrace the cold and enjoy the lack of emotions and embrace the cold as if welcoming home a long lost friend or family member.

Peace has yet to come; yet

Nothing is better than Something.

First Time

You make me smile with the simplest of words.

You make my heart falter with just a simple lift of your lips.

You make me want to do things I have never imagined I could do.

You make me feel special and wanted.

The way you worry about me is like I've never had someone do before.

I feel safe in your arms. I feel as an equal and not someone who is there for show.

You make me feel unique and special.

You make me feel vibrant and alive.

I have never known these feelings existed.

I read about them in books and from people speaking of them.

They have always been dreams and foreign to me.

I never knew I, too, could also know what these things were.

I never imagined I would ever experience them.

But just as I was losing hope that I would, you came along and wrecked my system like a storm off the gulf.

I can't go a day without thinking at least one thought of you.

You make my day seem so much brighter and able to carry on even in the darkest of hazes.

You are the first for me to not be able to see myself without.

I don't think I could have made it this far without you.

I knew all those times I almost ended and didn't was for a reason; I was meant to find you and you to find me.

It seems like we have been together for an eternity, when in reality; it has only been months.

I don't see me going on without you and I honestly do not want to.

You are the first for no regrets and no second thoughts.

You are stuck with me through it all.

I don't want any other than the one I have now.

You are my roots and blooming branches.

I see a future bright and full of color and love.

I can't wait to start anew with you, but then we already have started anew.

We have started to help each other heal and mend.

We have started to help each other become better than we were.

How?

How can one person be so bold as to tell the truth yet know that it will be considered a lie among all the other lies? How can one be so bold as to trust someone that they love yet know that the one they love is not as trust worthy as they seem? How can one be so bold as to stand up to those who hold the power to bring them down to their knees and hold them there till they scream for mercy? How can one be so bold as to let themselves be tortured till their soul is no more than a pile of dust in a cavity that once was a heart?

HOW CAN ONE BE SO BOLD?

I Am Omega

Our kind is rare in the world of hate

Peace is our goal for its power is great

The power of our love helps heal most wounds

Though others try to beat us down we still are strong

We don't last long under the tension of the world

Our faith and hope help us along

The forest is our comforting home and warm embrace

We falter when their hate filled eyes are fixed on us

We are sensitive not only in body but in mind as well

We are not the average being

We are....

Omegas

I Hate

I hate it when you do this.

I hate it when you don't.

I hate it when no one listens.

I hate it when someone thinks they
know me; but they don't.

I hate you for hating me

I hate this role you try to play with me

I hate to think about you

I hate not thinking about you

Innocent People

The lies that are told are unjust and
false;

The need for peace is strong, but weak
for most.

The pain of the lost suffocates all who
dwell on the past;

The need for forgiveness burns holes in
our hearts.

The longing for the future pushes us
forwards;

The hate in their eyes causes us to
cringe.

Last Chance

The breath of death rolls down my back.

It's getting colder and colder as I just sit and wait.

The icy fingers of her hand scrapes down my spine in a
seductive and taunting way.

She knows I'm near my limit; yet she also knows it's not
my time.

She just waits and watches; while I ponder and stew always
asking why.

She laughs cruelly at all the throws and punches aimed my
way.

Knowing that each one slowly and surely dents my armor
of faith and security.

My nerves get jumbled and strained.

Keeping me up at night; and having me hold my breath to
even think straight.

The hands on my arms shake from the self-restraints I use
to keep from lashing out at those who deal me pain.

My chest constricts with pain from holding back the tears
of broken friendships and truths told in vain.

Pain rips at my ribs as I fight to stay focused on what really
matters and keep the peace at all cost.

Is this worth it? For them to be happy and me to be in a
punishing, self-inflicted hell?

Can I truly last more days; months; even years?

That Death herself watches as she sees me writhe in self disappointment and pain.

She basks in the glory of my ever crumbling reality.

But wait; she will soon be growling in hatred and vain when he takes me away from the pain.

From the tears and heart ache.

He is my one and only; my lost love.

He is my saving grace and my glowing future.

He is my last chance at happiness.

Love Is Not Lost

My wounds have yet to heal

My world of Love incomplete

The space that was left now a cavern of despair

The life that had begun inside me, gone in a flash of pain

The essence of life that had once been now barley a whisper

My memories the only things left

The short while we had not enough

The Love will always be there

Lucky Stars

I thank my lucky stars for you. I never would have thought I could be so blessed as to have you by side and there for me when I needed you. I know we're apart and to tell ya the truth, that's okay because we're showing that even with distance; No one can tear us apart.

I thank my lucky stars for you. Cause you are the sunshine I feel on my face in the pouring rain. You are the breeze I feel on a hot summer day. The warmth of a burning fire on a cold winter's night. With you, all things seem to be so bright.

I thank my lucky stars for you. Because without you love, I wouldn't know how to say thanks. Without you the moon would be dull and the stars would be blank. If you had not found me, my hope would be but a tiny string floating away on the wind.

I thank my luck stars for you. Because with you, I'm happy to face the challenges ahead.

My Heart Is A Grenade

My heart can only hold SO MUCH PAIN until it blows up like a grenade in a battle field. The pieces are no longer able to be put back together for they are no longer there, they are just piles among piles of ash. The once beautiful canvas that was called me, no longer here or anywhere but floating around in the toxic air being breathed in by others of whom do not or did not want to know me. The pain is unbearable and the pressure the same as before. A stone weight sitting on my chest not allowing me to breathe without consequence. With just a single tug the string will release and everything will be gone. I will be gone. Nothing left except a pile of ash and charred pieces here and there. I am a grenade just waiting for the string to be pulled loose and set free.

My Last Moments

My heart is breaking and all I can do is wait for the pain to subside. I feel the pieces shattering, tiny piece by tiny piece. I feel them fall to the floor and I hear them plunk to their final resting place. My heart is no more. Nothing but a pile of broken pieces piled high on the floor in a mound of dirt. I see my soul hovering above it. It's light fading as I watch it rest above the broken pieces. It finally settles in the center of the pile of broken dreams and dirt. The light is gone and so is my heart. The pain from the hollowness in my chest is subtle but still there. My breath comes in raged waves. My pulse dimming to nothing. My life cut short by a stupid mistake. My light goes dim and bleary. My eyes focus on nothing but everything at once. The faces of those who I love, and who I thought were true the final images to race across my mind's eye. I fade into the dark. The Otherworld greets me with open arms and warm wishes. I am free at last! The pain of the hollowness cannot hurt me any longer. My heart is clean and pure. My wishes are true and my dreams anew.

My Tree

The leaves from My Tree float down and around me like a snow fall in winter.

I hear the voices of the forest calling to me.

The feel of the dirt under my bare feet is welcoming.

My hands reach out towards My Tree as it caresses my face.

The moss covered roots are summoning me to them and I willing comply to their request.

My mind is filled with the scents and sounds of Mother Earth as I sink down to the throne of moss and roots.

My body is released from the tension that had imprisoned it.

The feel of My Trees bark is comforting against my back.

The soft whisper of the creek running through My Tree is like a lullaby.

My Tree comforts me while I sleep in its embrace. It doesn't let anything interrupt me as I rest.

My Tree is more than a tree, it is a Warrior from Mother Earth herself.

The element of Life.

Nothingness

Missing people who can help make the pain and sorrow go
away.
Putting on the mask to help stay calm and level headed.
Putting up the walls to keep the pain and sorrow at bay.
Wearing the cloak of invisibility like a new fashion.
Drowning inside from all the tears I refuse to shed.
Hanging inside from the grief and mental pull of the
knowledge of what's to come.
Knowing it's never going to be the same again.
Holding onto the ledge, watching the skin on my fingers
peel off from holding too hard.
The dark oblivion waiting for me to let go.
Bloody drops beat me to it.
Let go.
Free fall.
No air.
No feeling.
Lifeless.
At peace.
The End.

Pain

Pain is something you feel when you're hurt or having too much fun. It doesn't feel very good and it doesn't feel right, but somehow you are always in pain. Whether it's mental pain or physical pain you always feel it. Pain can be from laughing to hard. It can be from being beat up. There's also pain that you feel when someone you love dies, or someone you love who doesn't love you treats someone better than they did you. Pain can be several types. Pain can be kind of good, and there's pain that can be bad. I don't like bad pain it makes me depressed. I like the kind of pain that you get when you're with a friend and you're laughing so hard it hurts. Pain is also something you feel when you find out that your baby died. Pain is so harsh that it can kill a person. Even if you don't think so it can defiantly kill a person. That's why pain is so harsh.

Peaceful As Death

The world slips from under me

The last feels of reality have long gone

The warmth has left and the cold has entered

The essence of Life is no more

The love that was is now not here

The healthy glow a dimmer

The light of the living has left

The dark of Death is here

The Other World awaits for me

The loved ones here are mourning

The longing to live is released in a breath

The peace of Death is warming

The soul stretches and makes its journey

The wait of longing is over

<u>Meet The Author</u>

Vala Boyd is a Celtic Norse pagan, who is originally from Texas and grew up in the Virginias' and Texas. She is a military brat who married an Army man, became a mama to two lil heathens and a homesteader
and rescuer to many animals. She is the main creator and the writer for her shop Through The Vail. Her hobbies include (and are not limited to) reading, photography, designing new items, and imagining all the wonderful fantasies she writes about and makes items for. She is a lover of cosplay and rein fairies and makes most of her garb from scratch or up-cycles.